Building The Perfect Team: What Staffing Skills Do IT Managers Need?

Tips And Techniques That IT Managers Can Use In Order To Correctly Staff Their Teams

"Practical, proven techniques that will help you to attract and retain the right staff"

Dr. Jim Anderson

Published by:
Blue Elephant Consulting
Tampa, Florida

Printed in the United States of America

Library of Congress Control Number: 2016918912

ISBN-13: 978-1539990987

ISBN-10: 1539990982

Warning – Disclaimer

Recent Books By The Author

Product Management

- Product Development Lessons For Product Managers: How Product Managers Can Create Successful Products

- Customer Lessons For Product Managers: Techniques For Product Managers To Better Understand What Their Customers Really Want

Public Speaking

- Delivering Excellence: How To Give Presentations That Make A Difference: Presentation techniques that will transform a speech into a memorable event

- How To Rehearse In Order To Give The Perfect Speech: How to effectively rehearse your next speech to that your message be remembered forever!

CIO Skills

- What CIOs Need To Know In Order To Successfully Manage An IT Department: Decision Making Skills That Every CIO Needs To Have In Order To Be Able To Make The Right Choices

- How CIOs Can Make Innovation Happen: Tips And Techniques For CIOs To Use In Order To Make Innovation Happen In Their

IT Department

IT Manager Skills

- Secrets Of Effective Leadership For IT Managers: Tips And Techniques That IT Managers Can Use In Order To Develop Leadership Skills

- IT Manager Career Secrets: Tips And Techniques That IT Managers Can Use In Order To Have A Successful Career

Negotiating

- Learn How To Argue In Your Next Negotiation: How To Develop The Skill Of Effective Arguing In A Negotiation In Order To Get The Best Possible Outcome

- How To Open Your Next Negotiation: How To Start A Negotiation In Order To Get The Best Possible Outcome

Miscellaneous

- Power Distribution Unit (PDU) Secrets: What Everyone Who Works In A Data Center Needs To Know!

- Making The Jump: How To Land Your Dream Job When You Get Out Of College!

Note: See a complete list of books by Dr. Jim Anderson at the back of this book.

Acknowledgements

Any book like this one is the result of years of real-world work experience. In my over 25 years of working for 7 different firms, I have met countless fantastic people and I've been mentored by some truly exceptional ones. Although I've probably forgotten some of the people who made me the person that I am today, here is my attempt to finally give them the recognition that they so truly deserve:

- Thomas P. Anderson
- Art Puett
- Bobbi Marshall
- Bob Boggs

Dr. Jim Anderson

This book is dedicated to my wife Lori. None of this would have been possible without her love and support.

Thanks for the best 21 years of my life (so far)...!

Speaking.   Negotiating.   Managing.   Marketing.

Table Of Contents

Team Building Is An IT Manager's #1 Job

An IT manager is only as good as his or her team is. This means that one of the most critical skills that an IT manager has is the ability to build the perfect team. The better a team that you can build, the better your team is going to make you look!

Building a world-class IT team starts with the recruiting process. You are going to have to understand the challenges associated with hiring the right people and what it takes to ensure that you have a truly diverse team. Where to look for the best candidates can be confusing, but often they are located locally.

Getting good people for your team is not all that you have to do. Once you've gotten them, you now have the responsibility of managing their expectations – which in some cases can be quite high. When people agree to join your team, they have expectations that you'll have their back when life's challenges come along and you need to be aware of these expectations.

No team is fixed, there are always changes happening. As a successful IT manager you are going to have to make sure that your staff are not planning on leaving you. You need to prevent staffing disasters before they occur. When people do leave, it presents you with an open positon on your team that you need to fill correctly.

Filling jobs starts with the same steps – creating an accurate job description that lays out what you are looking for in your candidates. It's going to be up to you to select the right person for the open job, but the challenge is that most of us have never had any training in how to do this correctly. The best way to avoid these challenges is to find ways to keep the staff that you have and understand why they might consider leaving you.

For more information on what it takes to be a great IT manager, check out my blog, The Accidental IT Leader, at:

www.TheAccidentalITLeader.com

Good luck!

- Dr. Jim Anderson

About The Author

I must confess that I never set out to be an IT manager. When I went to school, I studied Computer Science and thought that I'd get a nice job programming and that would be that. Well, at least part of that plan worked out!

My first job was working for Boeing on their F/A-18 fighter jet program. I spent my days programming fighter jet software in assembly language and I loved it. The U.S. government decided to save some money and went looking for other countries to sell this plane to. This put me into an unfamiliar role: I started to meet with foreign military officials and I ended up having to manage groups of engineers who were working on international projects.

Time moved on and so did I. I found myself working for Siemens, the big German telecommunications company. They were making phone switches and selling them to the seven U.S. phone companies. The problem was that the switches were too complicated. Customers couldn't tell the difference between one complicated phone switch from another complicated phone switch. Once again I found myself working with the sales and marketing teams to find ways to make the great technology that the engineers had developed understandable to both internal and external customers.

I've spent over 25 years working as an IT manager for both big companies and startups. This has given me an opportunity to learn what it takes to manage and IT teams in ways that allow them to maximize their output while becoming a valuable part of the overall company.

I now live in Tampa Florida where I spend my time managing my consulting business, Blue Elephant Consulting, teaching college courses at the University of South Florida, and traveling to work with companies like yours to share the knowledge that I have about how IT managers can become even more productive.

I'm always available to answer questions and I can be reached at:

Dr. Jim Anderson
Blue Elephant Consulting
Email: jim@BlueElephantConsulting.com
Facebook: http://goo.gl/1TVoK
Web: http://www.BlueElephantConsulting.com/

"Unforgettable communication skills that will set your ideas free..."

Create IT Departments That Are Productive And A Valuable Asset To The Rest Of The Company !

Dr. Jim Anderson is available to provide training and coaching on the topics that are the most important to people who have to manage IT departments: how can I build a productive IT department (and keep it together) while at the same time providing the rest of the company with the IT services that they need?

Dr. Anderson believes that in order to both learn and remember what he says, speakers need to laugh. Each one of his speeches is full of fun and humor so that what he says "sticks" with everyone.

Dr. Anderson's CIO Skills Training Includes:

1. How to identify and attract the right type of IT workers to your IT department.
2. How to build relationships with the company's senior management in order to get the support that you need?
3. How to stay on top of changing technology and security issues so that you never get surprised?

Dr. Jim Anderson works with over 100 customers per year. To invite Dr. Anderson to work with you, contact him at:

Phone: 813-418-6970 or
Email: jim@BlueElephantConsulting.com

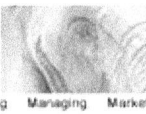

Blue
Elephant
Consulting
Speaking   Negotiating   Managing   Market

12

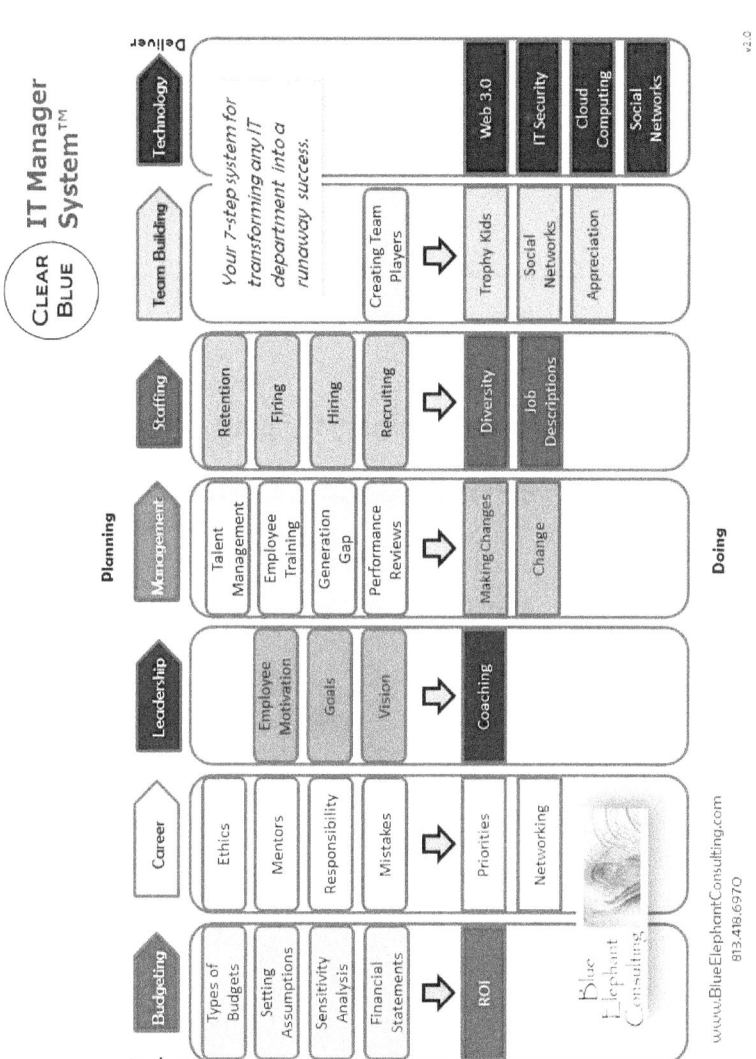

The **Clear Blue IT Manager System™** has been created to provide IT managers with a clear roadmap for how to manage an IT team. This system shows IT Managers what needs to be done and in what order to do it.

Chapter 1

Recruiting Is Something That IT Leaders Need To Start Thinking About Again

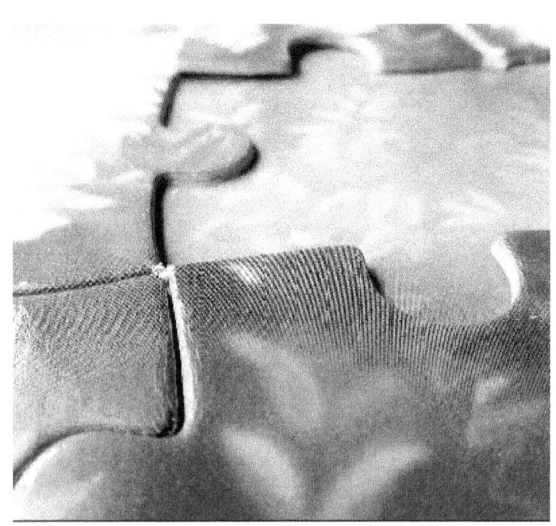

Chapter 1: Recruiting Is Something That IT Leaders Need To Start Thinking About Again

It's starting to look like the economic winter just might be getting ready to thaw. Once this happens, IT Leaders realize that they're going to have a massive task added to their already overloaded plate – recruitment.

During the economic downturn IT workers were staying put because they didn't know what was going to happen next. Additionally, firms stopped hiring except for the most critical functions. When things start to pick up again, **this will all change**. Are you going to be ready IT Leader?

The Problem With The Way That IT Recruits

We all need to remember that recruitment is really a game that we are playing with our competition – **we want to get all of the good talent** in order to boost our firm and our competition wants to do the same. On top of all of this, who among us has ever been trained on how to properly do recruitment?

The good folks over at Forrester Research realize that we need some help and so they've done some research for us. Their conclusions just might surprise you a bit. They believe that there is something that we need to start doing if we want to be successful in attracting the right kind of talent: we need to **diversify our talent pool**.

The Way That IT Recruiting SHOULD Be Done

Right now all of us pretty much do the same thing when we want to fill a position in our IT department: we start looking at other firms who do what we do in hopes of finding an IT professional who is willing to leave and come work for us.

This has worked for a long time because there have been so many people working in IT. However, with outsourcing and the Baby Boomers starting to retire, **this isn't going to keep working much longer**.

Instead, Forrester tells us that what we need to do is to expand the pool of talent that we recruit from when we go looking to fill a position. This means that we need to start looking at **college students** and **non-IT business professionals** as potential sources of new recruits.

College students have always been an **underused resource**. The reasons are many, but more often than not it boils down to the simple fact that it takes time to guide them when you give them a task – you can't just "fire and forget". Sometimes poor management of college student's results in poor performance and this can leave a lingering sense of frustration that causes IT Leaders to shy away from working with college students.

Non-IT business professionals, sometimes called "**super users**", are a fantastic under-tapped resource. This resource has both the technical and business knowledge that can prove invaluable to any IT department. Providing existing employees with an opportunity to rotate into the IT department can be a win-win situation: you get the talent that you need and the employee gets a brand new career track.

Final Thoughts

What are we really looking for when we go to fill an IT position? We'd really like to find candidates that have three things: **technical skills**, **business knowledge**, and **interpersonal skills**. The ponds that we've been fishing from for these types of workers has just about dried up. In order to meet the staffing challenges of the future, we're going to have to start fishing in other ponds.

Rethinking about how we attract, develop, and then retain college recruits can pay **huge dividends**. Who wouldn't want to hire someone that they already knew and who they had groomed for a specific role in the organization? Likewise inviting non-IT business professionals to join the IT department solves staffing problems and breaks down internal walls.

Learning to do a better job of fishing for new talent will mean that you will have found a way to transform yourself from an IT manager into a **true leader**.

Chapter 2

Staffing Diversity Challenges IT Leaders

Chapter 2: Staffing Diversity Challenges IT Leaders

They say that the world is becoming a smaller place – I think that they just might be right. IT Leaders are starting to realize that coming up with ways to staff their teams so that they **are diverse** is quickly moving from being a political nicety to now becoming a business necessity. Does anyone have any suggestions on how best to go about doing this?

The Problem

Most IT departments are no longer single site operations. In fact, with the growth of outsourcing a single IT department may now have offices in multiple countries: China, India, Russia, etc. This type of distributed operation is a great way to ensure that more work gets done at a lower price; however, it also poses a **significant staffing challenge** for IT Leaders.

It's all too easy to think that we can take a few high-performing IT Leaders from the U.S., plunk them down in one of our remote offices and have them become an effective leader. The reality is that all too often, this doesn't work. If you haven't **groomed someone** on your team to step in and run / interface with a remote office, then they aren't going to be able to do it.

In the U.S., IT managers are encouraged to use frank talk and direct confrontation in order to deal with team issues. However, especially when dealing with teams in Asia, this can come across as **being rude and offensive**.

What's An IT Leader To Do?

The trick to solving IT staffing challenges for remote offices or just to deal with remote offices is to create what the experts call a "**talent plan**". Doing this will allow you to provide unique levels of value to your remote IT offices.

The first part of a talent plan is to identify what positions on your team you are going to have to fill and what types of **cultural skills** those positions are going to require. It's important to note that it's not always necessary to hire a person of a given nationality in order to deal smoothly with a remote office that has other staff members of that nationality. Finding someone who is sensitive to that nationality and who has dealt with them before can fill this need.

Filling a position to manage a remote office should not be a sudden effort. IT Leaders realize that every position will eventually need to be filled because the person in that spot now will be promoted, let go, or will move on. A key part of any talent plan is to early on identify who the **potential replacements** are. This allows an IT Leader to take the time to make sure that the potentials get an opportunity to get trained in both the skills and the corporate values that they will need if they fill the position.

Final Thoughts

Staffing mistakes can be very expensive and picking the wrong person to lead a remote IT office or to interface with such an office can flat out be **disastrous**. IT Leaders realize that if they wait until the last minute when a position suddenly has to be filled, then it will be too late to do it correctly.

Instead, if they take the time to create a talent plan then their investment of upfront time and effort into **grooming** the right replacements will ensure that the correct staffing decisions are made. Learning to add diversity management to your IT team will mean that you will have found a way to transform yourself from an IT manager into a **true leader**.

Chapter 3

Tomorrow's IT Managers Can Be Found Locally

Chapter 3: Tomorrow's IT Managers Can Be Found Locally

Even in tough economic times, IT Leaders are still concerned about **losing talent**. Studies are showing that we are losing our IT Leaders at a much faster rate than new ones are being produced. On top of this, up to 30 million managers and leaders are going to become eligible to retire in the next five years. How can an IT Leader help to replace these leaders?

Defining The Problem

The loss of leaders in the IT field means that executive recruiters end up having to **move thousands of managers** not only cross-country but all between industries each year. This challenge has been complicated by what firms have been doing for the past few years.

In order to become leaner and reduce their operating costs, many firms have been **removing layers of IT management**. These tactics were a good idea when lean and nimble competition was showing up and taking business away from established firms. However, there has been a cost.

Those layers of IT management that have been removed used to provide **development opportunities** and ways for the next generation of IT leaders to grow. This has resulted in a situation where as the current crop of IT leaders get ready to roll off into retirement, there aren't enough replacement candidates waiting to take their place.

Solutions Start Locally

The key to solving this IT department staffing crisis is for IT Leaders to sit down with their HR departments and establish **good hiring practices** in their local branches. These practices need to create a good flow of diverse talent.

The goal must to be find ways to recruit and grow employees at the **local level**. Once this is done, then the future leaders can be fed into the company's core operations and this will provide a way to not only fill higher level positions but also solve the challenge of creating a diverse workforce.

Final Thoughts

Since we work in IT, we always look for a way to solve our problems using IT tools. Ensuring a steady flow of IT Leaders can be accomplished by creating an **automated tracking system** to identify those candidates who possess both the skills and the experience to handle new opportunities when they open up.

This type of system allows the firm to fill open IT positions much faster and with better suited candidates. If you can find a way to help your firm accomplish this, then you will have found a way to transform yourself from an IT manager into a **true leader**.

Chapter 4

Dealing With High Worker Expectations Requires Real IT Leadership

Chapter 4: Dealing With High Worker Expectations Requires Real IT Leadership

Can we talk frankly for just a moment? **Who's really in charge in IT** departments when it comes to hiring and retaining new talent? You'd think that with the global recession, companies would have the upper hand. However, with the critical importance of IT solutions to existing company operations and increasing global competition, it's possible that firms need IT workers more than IT workers need the firm. What's an IT leader to do?

My, How Things Have Changed!

How did we get to where we are today? It wasn't all that long ago that you could land a job in a company's IT department right out of college and then expect to spend either **your entire career** there or at least the next 10 years if you chose to do so. Those days are now long gone.

Instead, what we are dealing with today is workers who view their current jobs (or job opportunities) as relatively short lived events. The experts tell us that everyone needs to expect to have between **10-12 different jobs** during our IT careers. This new mindset makes it much harder for IT Leaders to recruit and retain the top IT talent that they need to move their teams forward faster.

New Solutions For IT Leaders

I've been hearing a lot IT managers lamenting the current state of recruiting top tier talent lately. To them I say "**get over it**". Look, the world is the way that it is and there's nothing that either you or I can do about it.

If new hires to your IT department are going to view their job as a temporary stop on their career journey, then fine – **work with it**. This simply means that you need to change how you manage your team.

In the past, IT managers were content to allow workers to "**niche**" and become experts in one particular area. No more. **Cross-training** of every member of your team should be among your highest priorities. This will benefit your team members because they will pick up new skills and won't get bored doing the same job over and over again. You'll benefit because when a team member decides to leave, the loss won't be quite as painful as it could be.

IT Leaders also need to be looking for **tomorrow's IT leaders**. A benefit of having a great deal of turnover in your teams is that you'll have a chance to evaluate a greater number of IT workers for future leadership positions. Those who have the necessary skills, are the ones that you need to give additional responsibilities to. By doing this, you just might convince them to stick around a bit longer...

Final Thoughts

The world has changed and IT Leaders need to **change along with it**. Coming to the realization that we **can't hope to keep** team members for extended periods of time means that we need to change how we hand out assignments and how we search for tomorrow's IT management talent. If you can adjust how you manage your teams to deal with the way that the world really is, then you will have found a way to transform yourself from an IT manager into a **true leader**.

Chapter 5

IT Leaders Deal With The Three D's: Death, Divorce, and Disease

Chapter 5: IT Leaders Deal With The Three D's: Death, Divorce, and Disease

Bad things happen. Sometimes they are not all that bad – key employees leaving for example is bad, but not really all that "bad". However, sometimes things really are bad: staff die or become seriously ill for long periods of time. What's your plan for when this happens? **What's that, you don't have a plan?** You think that it's the role of HR to take care of personal issues like this? Guess again...

Hey Pollyanna, Why Don't We Ever Plan For The Worst?

You would think that since we work in an industry that has spent so much time trying to prepare our IT systems to deal with bad things, that at least some of this careful planning **would have spilled over** into how we manage our IT teams. You would be wrong. Just like little kids, IT Leaders for some unknown reason can't imagine themselves or anyone on their staff dying (death), leaving (divorce), or getting seriously ill for a long time (disease).

One of the reasons that we never seem to get around to doing any proper succession planning is that we always seem to be **too focused on the here and now**. In order to plan for a future that has a different cast of characters in the IT department, IT Leaders need to sit down and do some serious thinking.

Why Bother Planning – Won't Things Just Change Anyway?

Sure we all know that just like motherhood and apple pie IT team succession planning is a good thing to do. But do we really know **WHY** it is a good thing to do? It turns out that there are two main reasons.

The first is the same problem that the U.S. faces with its 4-year presidential terms – **continuity of leadership**. Right now in your IT department you have plans that are asking for funding, you have plans that are underway, and hopefully you have plans that are just about to wrap up. If the firm loses key member(s) of the team or even you, then would these plans still complete successfully? Even if they did, would anyone have a clear idea of what to do next?

The second reason has to do with **intellectual property**. I speak from experience when I say that much of the value in any IT department is not in its written procedures or the code that lives on its servers, but rather what is in its employee's heads. If you lose one of these staff members, the IP loss could be staggering if you don't have a working succession plan in place.

What's The Right Way To Do IT Department Succession Planning?

Gary Perman is an IT consultant who has spent a great deal of time creating IT succession plans. From his vantage point all IT succession plans have **two key characteristics**:

Simplicity: A succession plan has got to be easy to use. When an individual is no longer available to do a job, then it has to be clear who has been trained to step into their spot. Oh, and it also has to be clear who will take things over for that person.

More Than A Replacement Plan: A succession plan can't just be a list of names. Instead it has to be a complete development plan that shows who is where in the skill development path that it is going to take in order to be ready to step into a particular role.

What All Of This Means To You

As an IT leader you've got to **anticipate changes** that will happen to your teams, including things happening to you. It is your responsibility to make sure that there is a plan in place to deal with the loss of any of your staff.

Since not everyone can do everyone else's job, this means that you've got to create a succession plan and then you've got to **publicize it**. This is not a place for secrets. Once you publicize it, you've got to make it everyone's responsibility to ensure that they are ready to step into the role(s) that they are slotted for.

You can help make this happen. Using techniques such as **cross-training and job rotation** will ensure that your staff will have an opportunity to develop all of the skills that they are going to need. Bad things happen, this doesn't mean that you can't be ready for them when they come.

Chapter 6

How To Keep Your Team From Leaving As The Economy Improves

Chapter 6: How To Keep Your Team From Leaving As The Economy Improves

I don't want to say that it's been easy to be an IT Leader during the recent global economic crisis. However, as the world economy tanked and countless people in all industries lost their jobs, the one thing that IT Leaders really didn't have to worry about was having members of their team jump ship to go to work for other firms – **there were no other jobs to be had**. Well as the economy improves, this is going to change. Got a plan for keeping your team on board?

Don't They Love Me? Why Would They Leave?

I've got an ugly history lesson for you – the experts tell us that when we've had a recession in the past, it's during the recovery that you'll see a big increase in people leaving your company for other career opportunities as more and more jobs **become available**.

So what's an IT Leader to do? The last thing that any one of us really wants to do is to provide our staff with the skills and training that will boost their ability (and desirability) to leave. However, **that's exactly what we should be doing**.

The Big Secret

Dr. Elizabeth Craig has been looking into this issue and she has made some surprising findings. What she's found is that the members of your team will stay longer if you actively work to provide them with the very skills that they are looking for to make themselves **more valuable in the job market**.

Specifically, what Dr. Craig says is that the IT Leaders who provide the members of their team with the most opportunities to **increase their value** in the marketplace will get the greatest benefit by doing so. This breakthrough realization is something that too few IT Leaders fully understand.

The Three Secrets To Retaining Your Team

As an IT Leader, you need to start to take action to retain your team before it's too late. There are **three specific steps** that you can take:

Grant New Responsibilities: especially in the world of IT, your team members really do want to be challenged. In surveys, team members reported that having the ability to work on tough problems and being given more responsibility are the #1 things that determines their level of career satisfaction.

Boost Skills: look, you've got smart people working as a part of your team right now. They realize that they don't know everything, but they have an unquenchable desire to learn more. You need to do what you can to help sate this need by providing your team with ways that they can learn more about things that are outside of their day-to-day jobs. In IT this especially includes providing the opportunity to learn more about how the company works and the basic underpinnings of business.

Networking: the ability to reach out and connect with others both inside and outside of the company is another critical desire on the part of your team members. Sure, their motivation may be to primarily build connections that could help them find their next job, but it will also help them gain fresh insights into how to solve the problems that they are working on right now.

When we were all children, one of the games that we used to play was called musical chairs. It involved constantly finding a new chair to sit in. As the global economy improves, the desire to play **musical careers** will start to seize your team and you could end up losing a lot of them.

It's difficult and costly to replace critical staff. You need to start **taking action right now** to retain your team. This means that you've got to provide them with new responsibilities, opportunities to broaden their skills, and ways to connect with more people both inside and outside of the company.

This all may seem **counterintuitive** to you – it's almost as though you are helping them to prepare to leave. However, this is not the case. It turns out that if you provide them with what they are truly looking for in their career, then although they could leave, they won't.

Chapter 7

How Do You Prevent A Staffing Disaster Before It Happens?

Chapter 7: How Do You Prevent A Staffing Disaster Before It Happens?

What do you think the mood of your IT team is right now? Poor? Downright bad? If your workplace is like most businesses out there right now, your team is still reeling from all of the layoffs, hiring freezes, pay cuts, etc. If nothing else, there has been a lingering sense of dread that has been in the air for the better part of two years. **What do you need to be doing?**

The Scope Of The Problem

There's nothing physically wrong with your team, they are just really, really **stressed out**. What this means is that their creativity and productivity are probably at all-time lows. You're going to need to step in and do something about this situation.

I can almost hear you now: "I just don't have time to do this right now." Well guess what, you had better start to find the time. Otherwise you are going to find yourself buried in **a wave of interviews** as you try to fill all of the open positions in your department when everyone leaves.

The Conference Board has done a survey of 5,000 U.S. households (your team may not have been part of the survey, but the results probably still apply) and the results showed that **only 45% were currently happy with their jobs**. You've got a problem on your hands.

Steps You Can Take Now To Avoid Problems Later

You've got no budget, you've got no open req's, what's an IT manager to do when you need to cheer up your team? The good news is that there are a lot of **low-cost, no-cost things** that you can do that will save you much grief later on:

Job Titles: What are the titles of your staff? They are probably pretty boring. One thing that you can do that costs no money is to look into upgrading their titles – titles only, no promotions. Yes, you'd have to work with HR to do this, but the joy of going from "Systems Engineer IV" to "Senior Systems Engineer" can be absolutely amazing.

Work Time Options: Is your current team working a forced 9-5 work day? Loosing up on this can be a great no-cost way to pump some life back into the department. Yes, the work still needs to be done and yes, the company still needs to get value for the paycheck that it's handing out; however, allowing your staff to determine when they work (including both nights and weekends) can go a long way to boosting morale and productivity. A nice side benefit of doing this is that it creates an almost entrepreneurial feeling and all of a sudden everyone becomes more willing to help each other out.

Bonuses: Remember when people used to get raises that were more than the cost of living? Well even though those days seem to long gone, one thing that you can do is to talk with HR and get your hands on some bonus money. Once you've got it, set up a bonus incentive program and just watch how everyone suddenly becomes motivated.

1-on-1 Meetings: This may be the simplest of all the things that you could do – start taking the time to listen. Set up a time once a week where you'll turn off the phone and the Instant Messaging and just talk with each staff members individually. This is a great chance for them to blow off steam, share their great new idea, or just have a chat with you. It doesn't have to be too long – 15 minutes will do just fine.

What All Of This Means For You

As the global economy starts to improve, you as an IT Leader are going to have to start taking steps to make your beaten down staff **feel special once again**. If you don't do this, then when the job market picks up, they are going to leave you.

Many of the most effective things that you can do involve **low-cost or no-cost actions**. Things like changing job titles, becoming more flexible with work times, or even just taking the time to listen better would all have positive results.

No matter what you decide to do, **make sure that you do something**. There is nothing more important for you to be spending your time on than making sure that your talented and experienced staff stay on board with you.

Chapter 8

The Secret To Filling An Open IT Position The Right Way

Chapter 8: The Secret To Filling An Open IT Position The Right Way

When you were just a worker-bee you didn't have to worry about things like hiring people – you just had to worry about hanging on to the job that you had. Now that you are an IT manager, you're going to have to start getting comfortable with your new role as someone who has to find people to fill open spots. Got any suggestions on how to do this correctly?

Step 1: Define The Job's Requirements

Although the ultimate goal of the hiring process is to find the right person for the job, you don't start out with people. Instead you need to start with the job.

You're going to have to sit down and take the time to lay out the job's requirements. You won't be able to even start the process of looking for someone to perform the job until after you make sure that you have a good understanding of just exactly what you are going to want them to be doing for you.

There are five different characteristics of a job description that you are going to have to document:

1. Primary responsibilities
2. Background needed
3. Personal characteristics
4. Organizational culture
5. Managerial style
6. Primary Responsibilities

In this part of a job description, you are going to want to identify the tasks that are involved in performing the job. Just as importantly, you may need to identify what tasks are not part of the job!

Background Needed

In your opinion, what kind of background is needed in order to successfully perform this type of job? Required background can include such things as college degrees, previous work experience, etc.

Personal Characteristics

This is where you start to really define what kind of person is going to be needed in order to perform this kind of job. One of the most important questions that you are going to have to specify for the job is if you need an extrovert or an introvert to fill the roll. Good people skills are not always needed if there is not a lot of contact with others required.

Organizational Culture

Every job exists within the company that created it. Every company has a different sense of corporate culture. Aspects of this culture that will impact the job can include things like how much teamwork is used to accomplish projects, how much conformity to company policies is required, and how rewards are handed out.

Management Style

In the end, how you manage will play a role in the type of person who will be best suited to fill this position. We all have different management styles and depending on our style, different types of workers will better suited to working for us.

What All Of This Means For You

One of the most critical jobs that an IT Leader has is hiring new workers to fill positions within the company. Before you can start the process of interviewing candidates, you need to first take the time to define the job's requirements.

When defining an IT job's requirements, you need to take into account a number of different factors. These include job responsibilities, background needed, personal characteristics, organizational culture, and your own management style.

Yes, this may seem like a lot of work to do up front when you have an open position on your team that you are trying to fill; however, the work is worth it. Knowing what job you are trying to fill is the key to finding the right person to do the work.

Chapter 9

How Do IT Leaders Write A Good Job Description?

Chapter 9: How Do IT Leaders Write A Good Job Description?

How would you like to end up spending the next year in court and costing your company many millions of dollars? Not a good way to manage your IT Leader career, eh? Too many of us risk doing this whenever we try to fill an IT position without first clearly defining what the job is...

Just Exactly What Is A Job Description?

A job description is exactly what it sounds like – a description of an IT job that you are trying to fill. The reasons that you create one are many and varied.

The primary reason for creating a job description is simply because although you know what you are looking for in a job candidate, the team of people who will actually help you find that person do not know. The other reason that creating a job description is so important is that should it become necessary to fire someone, a good job description is the key to protecting yourself from a lawsuit.

In most companies you won't be alone when you go to develop a job description. Your HR or legal departments probably already have a template for you to use. Just in case they don't (or if it is incomplete), here's what every job description should contain:

- Title of the job, what business unit it will be part of, and the name of the part of the company that it will belong to

- Responsibilities and assignments associated with the job

- Who the hiring manager is and which manager the job reports to (they are not always the same)

- A more detailed description of what the person who has the job will need to do including tasks, responsibilities, and perhaps even objectives for the job.

- How much they will be paid, where they need to perform the work, and what hours you expect them to work.

- What background is required to do the work such as college education, or previous work experience?

- Any personal characteristics that may be required (outgoing personality, good with people, etc.)

The Process Of Creating A Job Description

Sometimes we find ourselves in the position of creating a job description for a job that already exists – the person has just left. In these cases, you should not feel constrained by what the job was in the past when you are creating the job description. Instead, write the job description for what you want the next person to do for you – what the job should be going forward.

As you are writing the job description, you are going to have to be very careful about detailing the differences between what a candidate brings to the job. We all have different types of job knowledge, sets of skills, and personal abilities. Each job requires a unique set of these and when you are creating the job description you'll have to lay out what you are looking for.

Keep in mind that you are defining what you need to have the person that you hire do for you. If for some reason it turns out that they can't do the job, you are going to have to let them go. These situations can get out of hand quickly (and become expensive). In order to protect yourself and your company, make sure that the job description has enough detail so that you can clearly make a case if someone doesn't live up to your expectations.

Finally, a clearly written job description will keep you on the right side of the law. No matter what country you are in, having a job description that clearly states what you are looking for in a candidate will protect you from lawsuits from those whom you end up not hiring.

What All Of This Means For You

IT Leaders like to spend their time leading, charting new paths for their IT teams. Writing a job description may not seem like the best use of your time; however, it turns out that it is a crucial task to do and to do well.

When creating a job description, it's important to make sure that it contains at least the important pieces of information that we've detailed here. Additionally, you'll need to make sure to determine what skills are needed, what grounds for dismissal would be, and to be sure that you've covered all of the legal bases.

I'm not a lawyer and so you should be sure to talk to a lawyer when creating a job description. When you take the time to do this correctly, then you will have created a powerful document that will ensure that you get the right person for the job...

Chapter 10

How To Hire IT People: What They Never Told You

Chapter 10: How To Hire IT People: What They Never Told You

Congratulations – you're an IT leader. Now go hire someone. Wait a minute, did anyone ever take the time to tell you just exactly how you should go about hiring staff? I mean, you've been on the other side of the table when you were looking for a job, but what are you supposed to do differently when you are the one doing the hiring?

Where To Find People To Hire

All too often when you go looking for information on how to do a better job of hiring people, you'll run into a lot of rules about what NOT to do when you are hiring. All that legal stuff is important, but we're not going to talk about it here.

Instead, let's talk about where it all starts – finding people to hire. When a position opens up on your team, you'd like to think that the folks in the HR department will magically present you with a list of the best candidates, right?

The bad news here is that you are really the one who knows the most about what you are looking for. In order to be able to choose from the best group of candidates, you need to be the one who finds the best people to apply for your job.

This means that it's time for you to get out your network and start reaching out to both people that you know who could be good candidates as well as to people who might know people who should apply. Keep in mind that you don't really need a lot of people to apply for your job, just a few very good candidates will take care of your needs.

Once you've got a group of people who would like to be considered for your open position, very quickly you're going to be looking at a stack of resumes from these candidates. If you are not careful here, you may find yourself quickly overwhelmed.

If you've never been told what to look for in a resume, then the different formats and font styles may just cause you to become confused. What you really need here is a plan.

Your best approach is to use a two-pass method to process all of the resumes. The first pass should be a quick one and has a simple goal: you want to weed out the applicants who are clearly not qualified for the job. Make sure that you know what the minimum candidate qualifications are and get rid of any resume that doesn't meet all of these.

Your second pass is going to be more detailed. The good news is that your stack of resumes should be much smaller now. You are going to be looking for three things this time through:

Achievement: you are looking for candidates that have been successful in their past jobs. You want proof that they have been able to achieve clear results.

Matching Career Goals: does the job that you are trying to fill match with the next step on the candidate's career path? Would it be a step back or too much of a step up?

Good appearance: at this point in time, you've got nothing else to go on and so how the resume looks should convince you that this person is able to do good work.

When you are done with this pass, you want to walk away with a list of your top candidates that you want to move forward with and invite to do face-to-face interviews.

What All Of This Means For You

For IT Leaders, finding yourself on the other side of the table during the hiring process can come as quite a shock. If nobody has taken the time to explain to you how to do this, then you may end up not hiring the right people for the right job.

The responsibility for making sure that qualified candidates apply for your open position falls on your shoulders. Once you have a pile of resumes, using a two-pass process you can quickly process them and create a list of high quality candidates.

In order for an IT Leader to be successful, you're going to need to have the highest quality IT team supporting you. It's your responsibility to make sure that when you have an opening on your team, you do a good job of hiring someone to fill it. Use these suggestions and you'll find that the hiring process isn't as hard as it looks!

Chapter 11

IT Managers Need To Understand Why Staff Stay – And Why They Leave

Chapter 11: IT Managers Need To Understand Why Staff Stay – And Why They Leave

As an IT manager, your job is to lead a team and accomplish tasks. Sounds simple enough, doesn't it? You can only do this if the team that you are managing **stays together**. If people start to leave, it's disruptive when they leave and you are going to be distracted as you work to fill the open positions. It sure seems like you should have a good understanding of why members of your team will both stay and why they might leave...

Why Do People Stay In Their Job?

Sadly, there is **no one right answer** to the question of why IT workers stay in their job. Every one of us is different and we are all constantly dealing with an ever-changing set of life circumstances. These are the things that can cause enough pressure in our lives that will make leaving our current job seem like a valid choice.

As an IT manager, you need to understand why your staff **will stay with the company**. These are the things that you are going to want to spend your time making sure that they remain in place:

- **Company Pride:** it turns out that who we work for really does matter despite what we might say on a daily basis. When others ask us where we work, if the company has a good reputation and is looked up to, this will extend to your staff and they will be proud to tell others where they work. Working at an Enron or a Worldcom after they had been disgraced would have been a difficult place for IT staff to remain.

- **Manager Respect:** how your staff feels about you can be an incredibly powerful attraction force. If your staff feels that you support them and if they respect you, then they are going to be much more likely to stay in their current job. The good news about this is that this is the one retention force that you have the most control over – do this well and you'll be able to keep more of your staff on board.

- **Enough Compensation:** your team is giving their time and talents to the company. In return for this, they want to receive something in return. They will always be comparing the two – are they getting enough for what they are giving? Although in reality, your control over how much they get paid may be limited, you can control other aspects of their compensation (work start times, flex time, etc.) that will shape how they feel that they are being rewarded for their time and talent.

- **Type of work:** how a worker feels about the work that they are performing can have a big influence on their desire to stay or go. If they feel that their work is meaningful, then they'll stay. If they decide that their work doesn't matter or isn't having any impact on the world, then they'll be much more likely to leave and seek out more meaningful work.

Why Do People Stay In Their Job?

As an IT manager you are always going to be dealing with **the issue of having people leave the company**. Although you can't completely control this, you can at least be aware of the factors that can make it more likely that members of your team will leave.

IT managers who are aware of what makes workers leave are able to better work **to make sure that they don't**:

- **Changes In Company Leadership:** for a whole variety of reasons there can big changes that happen at the top your company. It can be caused by the sale of the company or just an unhappy board of directors. No matter the reason, nobody likes change.

  If your staff feel that the company is now going to be heading a different direction and they don't fully understand why, then they may decide to leave. Communication or the lack thereof can be a big part of this leaving factor.

- **Conflict With Managers:** one of the most powerful reasons for people to leave the firm is because they are not getting along with their manager. No matter how wonderful the rest of the company is, this every-day type of conflict can override everything else and cause people to leave.

- **Friends Leave:** every team is a collection of relationships. When a worker's friends leave the company, that worker's network of relationships is damaged and if there is not enough of a network left, then there's a good chance that the worker may leave.

- **Work-life balance issues:** every team member has a life outside of work. If work starts to interfere with how a person is living their life, then there is going to be conflict that may end up in making the person have to make a choice between work and other activities. Work often loses this battle.

What All Of This Means For You

As an IT manager you need a team in order to accomplish your goals. Every member of your team will constantly be making judgements as to if they should remain in their job **or move on to another job**.

IT managers **need to understand** what will make their staff stay in their jobs. At the same time, managers need to also understand the forces that can cause team members to decide to leave the team.

We've identified **the major forces** that you are going to have to be aware of in order to keep your team together. Although you can't control everything, staying on top of these issues allows an IT manager to keep your team together and on track.

Chapter 12

How Are IT Managers Supposed To Keep Their Best Employees?

Chapter 12: How Are IT Managers Supposed To Keep Their Best Employees?

When I talk with new IT managers, more often than not they tell me that their biggest challenge is getting good at hiring the right people for their teams. One of the reasons that this is so challenging is because it's new to them. What they don't know yet, is that hiring is only one side of the coin – retaining your staff is the other side and it turns that this can be an even bigger challenge.

You Are Going To Lose People

Can we talk frankly for just a minute? Do you really think that your magical IT management skills are going to keep your entire team together for as long as you work at your company? I can answer this question for you: no. You need to anticipate that you are going to be having people leave your team all the time. A good rule of thumb is to expect a turnover rate of about 15% per year. The math is pretty simple: for a team of 10 people you'll lose 1-2 people per year, for a team of 20 people you'll lose 3 people per year.

Remember that the rate that you lose people at may have nothing to do with your management abilities. The overall economy (both when it's up and when it's down) can have a big impact on how many people choose to leave your team each year.

During tough economic times, the number of people who leave your team will go down dramatically. However, this will all balance out because when the economy improves in the future you'll lose more than your share of staff.

Why Bother With Retention?

So you are going to lose people – so what? You can't prevent people from leaving, so is it really worth your time to try and keep people on board? The answer to this question turns out to be "yes, it is worth it".

When a member of your team walks out the door, you are losing much more than just a set of hands – you are also losing a brain. In that brain is the knowledge of how your company does business. This so-called "intellectual property" (IP) is what makes your department / company different from every other IT department / company out there. An additional challenge is that if a team member leaves and goes to one of your competitors then all of sudden you may be competing with yourself.

Keeping your internal and external customers happy is what every IT manager wants to do. Since you are not the only one on your team who has contact with customers, you need to make sure that your team is happy and satisfied so that when they interact with customers they provide good customer service. Happy staff don't leave, unhappy staff do. Keeping everyone happy and delivering great customer service is just one part of a solid retention strategy.

Finally, it's really expensive to have staff leave your team. You might think that having someone leave will save you money, but it's not true. Let's look at how this is going to end up costing you money.

First, there's going to be costs that will go along with the process of hiring someone to replace the person who has left. Next there are the indirect costs that have to do with the impact that losing a member of your team will have: more work for everyone else to do, impact on morale, and the potential that it will cause others to leave also. Finally, you need to account for the opportunity costs that having a smaller team will cause. You won't be able to take on as much work nor will you be able to complete tasks as quickly as you might like to. This will all result in missed revenue and increased costs.

What All Of This Means For You

Forget all of the technical design and implementation tasks that you have to do as an IT manager. You need to understand that getting your team staffed and then keeping it staffed at full strength is a key part of what being an IT manager is all about.

Staff retention can seem like a burden for an overworked IT manager. However, it's a very important part of the job. Losing a member of your team can result in three types of costs for the company: direct costs of interviewing new candidates, indirect costs of overworked remaining team members, and opportunity costs for missed deadlines and work that can't be taken on.

There's an old saying that goes "an ounce of prevention is worth a pound of cure". This is relevant to our discussion because if you take the time and make the effort to retain your IT team members, then you'll be able to accomplish more and will end being a more successful IT manager.

It's from the forge of failure that the steel of success is formed.

Hard Work Does Not Guarantee Success, But Success Does Not Happen Without Hard Work.

- Dr. Jim Anderson

Create IT Departments That Are Productive And A Valuable Asset To The Rest Of The Company !

Dr. Jim Anderson is available to provide training and coaching on the topics that are the most important to people who have to manage IT departments: how can I build a productive IT department (and keep it together) while at the same time providing the rest of the company with the IT services that they need?

Dr. Anderson believes that in order to both learn and remember what he says, speakers need to laugh. Each one of his speeches is full of fun and humor so that what he says "sticks" with everyone.

Dr. Anderson's CIO Skills Training Includes:

1. How to identify and attract the right type of IT workers to your IT department.
2. How to build relationships with the company's senior management in order to get the support that you need?
3. How to stay on top of changing technology and security issues so that you never get surprised?

Dr. Jim Anderson works with over 100 customers per year. To invite Dr. Anderson to work with you, contact him at:

Phone: 813-418-6970 or
Email: jim@BlueElephantConsulting.com

Blue
Elephant
Consulting
Speaking   Negotiating   Managing   Market

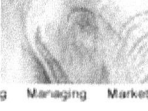

Photo Credits:

Cover - Gianpiero Addis
https://www.flickr.com/photos/punkjazz/

Chapter 1 - Yasmeen
https://www.flickr.com/photos/59152532@N05/

Chapter 2 - Oregon Department of Transportation
https://www.flickr.com/photos/oregondot/

Chapter 3 - Christoph Hensch
https://www.flickr.com/photos/cmhensch/

Chapter 4 - Molly Sabourin
https://www.flickr.com/photos/mollysabourin/

Chapter 5 - duncan c
https://www.flickr.com/photos/duncan/8427490505/

Chapter 6 - U.S. Pacific Fleet
https://www.flickr.com/photos/compacflt/

Chapter 7 - Chris Betcher
https://www.flickr.com/photos/betchaboy/

Chapter 8 - Brenda Gottsabend
https://www.flickr.com/photos/gottgraphicsdesign/

Chapter 9 – BookMama
https://www.flickr.com/photos/myloonyland/

Chapter 10 - Gangplank HQ
https://www.flickr.com/photos/gangplankhq/

Chapter 11 - Emilio Labrador
https://www.flickr.com/photos/3059349393/

Chapter 12 - Jobs For Felons Hub
https://www.flickr.com/photos/144110575@N07/

Other Books By The Author

Product Management

- How To Create A Successful Product That Customers Will Want: Techniques For Product Managers To Boost Product Sales And Increase Customer Satisfaction

- What Product Managers Need To Know About World-Class Product Development: How Product Managers Can Create Successful Products

- How Product Managers Can Learn To Understand Their Customers: Techniques For Product Managers To Better Understand What Their Customers Really Want

- Product Management Secrets: Techniques For Product Managers To Boost Product Sales And Increase Customer Satisfaction

- Product Development Lessons For Product Managers: How Product Managers Can Create Successful Products

- Customer Lessons For Product Managers: Techniques For Product Managers To Better Understand What Their Customers Really Want

- Product Failure Lessons For Product Managers: Examples Of Products That Have Failed For Product Managers To Learn From

- Communication Skills For Product Managers: The Communication Skills That Product Managers Need To Know How To Use In Order To Have A Successful Product

- How To Have A Successful Product Manager Career: The Things That You Need To Be Doing TODAY In Order To Have A Successful Product Manager Career

- Product Manager Product Success: How to keep your product on track and make it become a success

Public Speaking

- Delivering Excellence: How To Give Presentations That Make A Difference: Presentation techniques that will transform a speech into a memorable event

- Tools Speakers Need In Order To Give The Perfect Speech: What tools to use to create your next speech so that your message will be remembered forever!

- How To Create A Speech That Will Be Remembered

- Secrets To Organizing A Speech For Maximum Impact: How to put together a speech that will capture and hold your audience's attention

- How To Become A Better Speaker By Changing How You Speak: Change techniques that will transform a speech into a memorable event

- How To Give A Great Presentation: Presentation techniques that will transform a speech into a memorable event

- How To Rehearse In Order To Give The Perfect Speech: How to effectively rehearse your next speech to that your message be remembered forever!

- Secrets To Creating The Perfect Speech: How to create a speech that will make your message be remembered forever!

- Secrets To Organizing The Perfect Speech: How to organize the best speech of your life!

- Secrets To Planning The Perfect Speech: How to plan to give the best speech of your life

- How To Show What You Mean During A Presentation: How to use visual techniques to transform a speech into a memorable event

CIO Skills

- What CIOs Need To Know In Order To Successfully Manage An IT Department: Decision Making Skills That Every CIO Needs To Have In Order To Be Able To Make The Right Choices

- Becoming A Powerful And Effective Leader: Tips And Techniques That IT Managers Can Use In Order To Develop Leadership Skills

- CIO Secrets For Growing Innovation: Tips And Techniques For CIOs To Use In Order To Make Innovation Happen In Their IT Department

- Your Success As A CIO Depends On How Well You Communicate: Tips And Techniques For CIOs To Use In Order To Become Better Communicators

- What CIOs Need To Know About Working With Partners: Techniques For CIOs To Use In Order To Be Able To Successfully Work With Partners

- Critical CIO Management Skills: Decision Making Skills That Every CIO Needs To Have In Order To Be Able To Make The Right Choices

- How CIOs Can Make Innovation Happen: Tips And Techniques For CIOs To Use In Order To Make Innovation Happen In Their IT Department

- CIO Communication Skills Secrets: Tips And Techniques For CIOs To Use In Order To Become Better Communicators

- Managing Your CIO Career: Steps That CIOs Have To Take In Order To Have A Long And Successful Career

- CIO Business Skills: How CIOs can work effectively with the rest of the company!

IT Manager Skills

- Save Yourself, Save Your Job – How To Manage Your IT Career: Secrets That IT Managers Can Use In Order To Have A Successful Career

- Growing Your CIO Career: How CIOs Can Work With The Entire Company In Order To Be Successful

- How IT Managers Can Make Innovation Happen: Tips And Techniques For IT Managers To Use In Order To Make Innovation Happen In Their Teams

- Staffing Skills IT Managers Must Have: Tips And Techniques That IT Managers Can Use In Order To Correctly Staff Their Teams

- Secrets Of Effective Leadership For IT Managers: Tips And Techniques That IT Managers Can Use In Order To Develop Leadership Skills

- IT Manager Career Secrets: Tips And Techniques That IT Managers Can Use In Order To Have A Successful Career

- IT Manager Budgeting Skills: How IT Managers Can Request, Manage, Use, And Track Their Funding

- Secrets Of Managing Budgets: What IT Managers Need To Know In Order To Understand How Their Company Uses Money

Negotiating

- Learn How To Signal In Your Next Negotiation: How To Develop The Skill Of Effective Signaling In A Negotiation In Order To Get The Best Possible Outcome

- Learn The Skill Of Exploring In A Negotiation: How To Develop The Skill Of Exploring What Is Possible In A Negotiation In Order To Reach The Best Possible Deal

- Learn How To Argue In Your Next Negotiation: How To Develop The Skill Of Effective Arguing In A Negotiation In Order To Get The Best Possible Outcome|

- How To Open Your Next Negotiation: How To Start A Negotiation In Order To Get The Best Possible Outcome

- Preparing For Your Next Negotiation: What You Need To Do BEFORE A Negotiation Starts In Order To Get The Best Possible Deal

- Learn How To Package Trades In Your Next Negotiation

- All Good Things Come To An End: How To Close A Negotiation - How To Develop The Skill Of Closing

In Order To Get The Best Possible Outcome From A Negotiation

- Take No Prisoners In Your Next Negotiation: How To Start A Negotiation In Order To Get The Best Possible Outcome

Miscellaneous

- How Software Defined Networking (SDN) Is Going To Change Your World Forever: The Revolution In Network Design And How It Affects You

- The Power Of Virtualization: How It Affects Memory, Servers, and Storage: The Revolution In Creating Virtual Devices And How It Affects You

- The Internet-Enabled Successful School District Superintendent: How To Use The Internet To Boost Parental Involvement In Your Schools

- Power Distribution Unit (PDU) Secrets: What Everyone Who Works In A Data Center Needs To Know!

- Making The Jump: How To Land Your Dream Job When You Get Out Of College!

- How To Use The Internet To Create Successful Students And Involved Parents

"Tips And Techniques That IT Managers Can Use In Order To Correctly Staff Their Teams"

> This book has been written with one goal in mind – to show you how an IT manager can attract and retain the right staff. It's not easy being an IT manager so we're going to show you what you need to be doing in order to hire and motivate the team that will make you successful!
>
> **Let's Make Your IT Career A Success!**

What You'll Find Inside:

- **IT LEADERS DEAL WITH THE THREE D'S: DEATH, DIVORCE, AND DISEASE**

- **HOW TO KEEP YOUR TEAM FROM LEAVING AS THE ECONOMY IMPROVES**

- **HOW DO IT LEADERS WRITE A GOOD JOB DESCRIPTION?**

- **HOW TO HIRE IT PEOPLE: WHAT THEY NEVER TOLD YOU**

Dr. Jim Anderson brings his 25 years of real-world experience to this book. He's been an IT manager at some of the world's largest firms. He's going to show you what you need to do (and not do!) in order to successfully manage your career!

www.ingramcontent.com/pod-product-compliance
Lightning Source LLC
Chambersburg PA
CBHW061202180526
45170CB00002B/916